# TUDOR ENGLAND

ASHMOLEAN MUSEUM PUBLICATIONS

ARCHAEOLOGY, HISTORY AND CLASSICAL STUDIES

© Text and illustrations copyright the University of Oxford,
Ashmolean Museum, Oxford 2000
All rights reserved

ISBN 1 85444 140 X

BRITISH LIBRARY CATALOGUING-IN-PUBLICATION DATA
A catalogue record for this publication is available from the British Library

Designed and typeset by Andrew Ivett
Printed and bound in Singapore by Craftprint International Ltd.

UNIVERSITY OF OXFORD
ASHMOLEAN MUSEUM

# TUDOR ENGLAND

Archaeological and Decorative Art Collections
in the Ashmolean Museum
from Henry VII to Elizabeth I

by

**MOIRA HOOK**
and
**ARTHUR MacGREGOR**

ASHMOLEAN MUSEUM · OXFORD
2000

# CONTENTS

# ACKNOWLEDGEMENTS

We are grateful to Professor Diarmaid MacCulloch, who read the text in draft and who made many valuable comments. The photographs are for the most part by Nick Pollard, with others by his colleagues in the Ashmolean's photographic studio, David Gower, Jane Inskipp and Anne Holly. Figures 29 and 30 are reproduced by courtesy of the Bodleian Library, University of Oxford.

# ENGLAND'S TUDOR RENAISSANCE

At the death of the last Plantagenet king, Richard III, on Bosworth Field on 22 August 1485, the throne of England was claimed by Henry Tudor, Earl of Richmond. Henry's right of accession was questionable and his coronation was hastily concluded lest other claimants came forward. This act of presenting the nation's representatives with a *fait accompli* revealed a mature sensitivity to the problems that were to haunt his reign, but Henry VII was to bring to England a stability and peace unknown during the thirty turbulent years of the Wars of the Roses. Astute and firm, though sometimes judged obsessive and avaricious, Henry brought to the throne the kind of qualities that the country badly needed. He was shrewd enough to appease the Yorkists by marrying Elizabeth of York, eldest daughter of Edward IV and his Queen Elizabeth Woodville. He created dynastic links with Spain and Scotland. A marriage was concluded between his eldest son, Prince Arthur and Catherine of Aragon, but when Arthur died five months after the wedding in 1502, Henry salvaged the union with Spain by proposing that Catherine should now marry his second son, the future Henry VIII. His elder daughter Margaret, meanwhile, was married to James IV of Scotland, a union that was to have repercussions for the succession a century later. Ironically, although Henry VII is often remembered for his parsimony, it is by way of the coinage that the earliest blossoming in England of European Renaissance ideas can be demonstrated. In 1504 the first testoon or shilling was struck: the new coin carried a true portrait of the king on the obverse, the first English coin to do so, following a trend towards more realistic portraiture that had begun in Italy a generation or so earlier.

By the time of Henry VII's death, after twenty-five years of peace at home and no costly war abroad, the country was left with a buoyant and stable economy. Most importantly, the Tudor dynasty had an undisputed successor in the accomplished person of the eighteen-year-old Henry VIII. A serious scholar, a prodigious sportsman and talented musician, and having inherited a fortune from his father, Henry was said to be the most personable prince in Europe. He loved hunting and tennis among other physical activities and at the same time was a student of theology and a patron of the arts. Having very different qualities from his father, Henry chose, in the early years of his reign, to spend much of his time in these courtly pastimes, although he never totally relinquished his role as a policy-maker. From the start of his reign he took the

**Fig. 1. PORTRAIT OF ELIZABETH WOODVILLE (by an unknown artist.) Elizabeth Woodville was married privately to Edward IV in 1464. Henry VII married their daughter Elizabeth of York, thus uniting the erstwhile warring factions of Lancaster and York. She was therefore the mother-in-law of Henry VII and the grandmother of Henry VIII.**

**Fig. 2. TESTOON OF HENRY VII, 1504.** The testoon or shilling, a silver coin weighing 144 grains and worth 12 pence, tariffed at 20 shillings to the sovereign (£1). This was a new coin that, for the first time, attempted to depict a true likeness of the monarch. The reverse is inscribed with a cross over Tudor arms and surrounded by the Latin motto *Posui Deum Adiutorem Meum* (I have made God my Helper).

important decisions but always relied on able and well-chosen ministers to deal with the administration and financing of such policies. Love of pomp and show led to his spending less wisely than his father had and he entered into expensive wars both with Scotland and France. In his French adventures Henry began as a pawn in the Spanish king's game but he learned quickly to change sides when it suited him. A separate negotiated peace treaty with France was sealed by the marriage of Henry's younger sister Mary to Louis XII of France. The Scottish war had devastating results for the northern neighbour at Flodden with the death of James IV and the accession of the infant James V, whose mother was Margaret, Henry VIII's other sister.

Dynastic preoccupations weighed heavily on Henry's mind; the marriage to Catherine of Aragon failed to produce a male heir and in his subsequent pursuit of an annulment Henry met not acquiescence but opposition. Catherine's resistance was perhaps the most important factor in bringing the Reformation to England and ultimately in the break with the Church of Rome.

With his wide interests and talents, Henry was the embodiment of Renaissance princely ideals. His encouragement of new learning and the arts, as well

as his laying the foundations for the Royal Navy, increased the prestige of England as a European power. His matrimonial upheavals, however, continued to the end of his life. Two of Henry's six wives were beheaded, two had their marriages declared null, one died and one survived him. As the reign proceeded the regal fortitude of the young prince gave way to resolute wilfulness and irascibility as Henry aged into an autocratic tyrant.

The three children born to Henry came from the first three of his six marriages. His only son, Edward VI born in 1537 to Jane Seymour, was younger than the two sisters who were to succeed him in turn after Edward's short reign of only six years (1547–53). Mary I (ruled 1553–58), the daughter of Henry's first wife Catherine of Aragon, earned the nickname 'Bloody Mary' for the way she persecuted Protestants in her zeal to reclaim the country for Catholicism. Mary's marriage to Philip of Spain was short-lived and produced no heir; at the end of her brief and unhappy reign Mary was forced to acknowledge her sister Elizabeth, daughter of the ill-fated Ann Boleyn

In Elizabeth I (ruled 1558–1603) England was fortunate to find a Tudor monarch of remarkable ability. Possessing many of her father's better qualities and enjoying many of the same interests, Elizabeth was popular and successful throughout her forty-five year reign, regarded as a golden era for England when a new spirit of national identity coincided with a period of internal peace.

The arts flourished with a new zest. The spirit of the Elizabethan age is reflected in the flowering of the theatre, culminating in the drama of William Shakespeare. Freed from costly military adventures, national energy was concentrated on exploiting a new-found maritime advantage which challenged the might of Spain and established the sea routes that were to provide opportunities for long-distance trade and colonisation. Under the growing influence of continental Renaissance ideals a strong desire for education arose and as scientific knowledge expanded practical benefits accrued. The firearms and cannon that had been developed in her father's reign provided Elizabeth's galleons with a fire-power at sea to match the skill of her seamen. Having given her life to her country but never having married, Elizabeth was forced to acknowledge the Stuart succession: the great-grandson of Henry VII, in the person of James VI of Scotland, brought an end to Tudor rule in England when he succeeded to the throne in 1603 as the first monarch of the Stuart dynasty.

**Fig. 3. GROAT OF HENRY VIII, 1544–7.** The silver coinage of the last years of Henry's reign was progressively debased. The coins bear a facing bust of a portly, debauched king, far-removed from the handsome prince displayed on his earliest coins.

**Fig. 4. QUEEN ELIZABETH'S SEAL.** This wax impression made from the reverse of Queen Elizabeth's Second Great Seal, designed by Nicholas Hilliard, shows the Queen on horseback wearing a fashionable coif beneath her crown, her formal dress set off with a stiff collar. As well as the Tudor rose, the seal bears the emblems of France and Ireland: in reality one had already been lost to the English crown and its claim to the other is still being disputed today.

Fig. 5. *DEATH LEADING A PAGAN WOMAN*. A painted plaster panel salvaged from a house in Broad Street, Oxford, where it formed part of a cycle of related images; later repainting based on a sixteenth-century original. During the Middle Ages, the *Dance of Death* (or *danse macabre*) was occasionally acted-out, during the performance of which the character of Death seized onlookers one after the other without distinction of class or privilege. The theme became popular in northern Europe when Hans Holbein the Younger (1497–1543) made a noted series of engravings of the dance, showing a skeletal figure surprising his victims in the midst of their daily life.

# REFORMATION AND COUNTER REFORMATION

During the sixteenth century a growing dissatisfaction with the Church of Rome emerged among certain educated scholars and clergy. Popes, cardinals and archbishops lived like great princes, worship seemed riddled with superstition and fear, bishoprics and indulgences could be bought and sold. At the same time the poor and uneducated, constantly reminded that they should repent and pay for their sins by giving to the Church, lived in fear of Hell and damnation or the pains of Purgatory as depicted in the graphic illustrations which decorated their churches. Many English people, however, while disliking the ways of their clergy and having little love for the papacy in Rome, remained content to submit to the orthodoxy of the Church's doctrine.

On the Continent the Reformation crystallized around the writings and protestations of individual scholars like Desiderius Erasmus, Martin Luther and John Calvin. Erasmus of Rotterdam spent a number of years in England; Sir Thomas More fell under his influence, but although both men shared beliefs and yearned for radical reform, neither wished to break with the Church. Throughout England the Reformation took root in a haphazard manner and at times for reasons other than deep religious fervour. Henry VIII himself responded critically to the writings of Luther and was rewarded with the title of Defender of the Faith by a grateful Pope Leo X.

The most powerful prelate in the land was Thomas Wolsey, appointed Lord Chancellor by Henry VIII in 1515, the same year that the Pope elevated him to the office of Cardinal. From humble beginnings his natural ability and dedication to his career carried him to heights where his wealth and power seemed to equal that of the King. In the administration of his twin offices he sought to please both King and Pope, but Henry VIII's wish to have his marriage to Catherine of Aragon declared null, in order to marry Anne Boleyn, intervened to provoke a dilemma for Wolsey and to hasten the onset of the Reformation in England. Henry needed the help of Wolsey, who as Papal Legate was required to get a favourable judgement from Rome. Protracted negotiations concerning the annulment of the marriage did not please Henry, while Wolsey's many enemies were only too ready to speak up against him. As a result Wolsey lost his power as well as much of his wealth and was banished to York, where he remained Archbishop (though hitherto he had never so much as visited the city). Within a year he was dead.

Although a devout Catholic, Henry turned to new ministers to help engineer the break with Rome. Both Thomas Cromwell, the new chief minister, and Thomas Cranmer, Archbishop of Canterbury were supporters of the new Protestant teaching and were willing allies. Between 1532 and 1534 Parliament passed a number of Acts, as a result

**Fig. 6. THOMAS WOLSEY, engraved portrait after a painting by Hans Holbein.**

Fig. 7. 'CRANMER'S BAND'. This hinged iron band with lockable shackle is said to have been worn around the waist by Archbishop Cranmer during his confinement in Oxford in 1554.

of which Henry repudiated the authority of Pope Clement VII and attained supremacy over the new Church of England. Now that the Crown had officially broken from the Church of Rome, existing discontents among ordinary people with that church and its clergy were given legitimacy and the Reformation in England was gradually accepted.

As Supreme Head of the Church of England, Henry VIII was aware that the inhabitants of the many monasteries and nunneries scattered throughout England were part of an international system which might encourage allegiance to the Pope. Monasticism was vulnerable to attack, for although many houses were effective enough communities, some had declined to a handful of souls – popularly portrayed as living in a luxurious manner at odds with their vows of poverty and chastity. Except in the north of England, Henry's dissolution of these monasteries was carried through with little internal resistance; between 1536 and 1540 over 800 religious houses were dissolved, their assets seized by the Crown and their inhabitants dispersed. The King plundered the altar plate and other treasures; the buildings were quarried for their stone or converted to other uses and the estates were granted or sold off to the nobility and gentry. Vast tracts of England were released from Church ownership in this way and re-entered the private domain.

Edward VI's reign saw the consolidation of a growing Reformation. The young King's counsellors were strongly Protestant; under their influence the reforms instituted by his father were prosecuted with continuing zeal. Cranmer's English *Book of Common Prayer,* first published in 1549, encouraged a new identity between the English people, church and state. England had not only broken from Rome but had discarded totally the Catholic style of religion. When Edward died aged sixteen, ending a reign too short to eliminate all Catholic following, there were fears that if his sister Mary Tudor succeeded to the throne the country would revert to the old religion. To avoid this possibility the Duke of Northumberland tried to by-pass Mary in favour of Lady Jane Grey: she was the granddaughter of the younger of Henry VII's daughters, who had married the Duke of Suffolk after a brief union with Louis XII. This ill-fated attempt failed in the face of popular opinion that Mary Tudor, as the rightful heir, should succeed.

Two aims dominated Mary's ambitions when she came to the throne and her single-mindedness in pursuing them was to weaken the initial popularity which she enjoyed: these were to restore England to the Catholic religion and to re-impose obedience to Rome. Proud of her Spanish descent, she wished to reinforce dynastic links

Fig. 8. SILVER COMMUNION CUP, 1565, maker's mark *IC*. Under Archbishop Parker a concerted campaign was mounted in the 1560s to convert all medieval chalices in parish churches into 'decent' communion cups. This was done to emphasize the break with the past and to provide a cup with a larger capacity, consonant with the extension of communion to the laity under the new Protestant liturgy.

**Fig. 9. GOLD MEDAL OF HENRY VIII, 1545.** Struck to commemorate Henry's proclamation as head of the Church of England ten years previously. The legend translates 'Henry VIII, King of England, France and Ireland, Defender of the Faith and Under Christ the Supreme Head of the Church of England and Ireland'.

through her marriage to Philip of Spain, who succeeded his father Emperor Charles V in 1455. Although Mary may have been no more lacking in personal compassion than any of her Tudor predecessors, she is best remembered for having almost 300 Protestants burned at the stake. In Oxford, Bishops Hugh Latimer and Nicholas Ridley were burned in October 1555, followed by Archbishop Thomas Cranmer after he had first recanted the Protestant faith and then revoked his recantation in March 1556. When Mary Tudor died in 1558 her attempt to bring about a Counter Reformation was brought to an end.

On her accession, Elizabeth I and her advisers followed a path of compromise rather than confrontation. The Church of England retained some of the style of the Catholic faith in its liturgy, the Church retained the office of bishop, and churches that had for centuries formed the focal points of communities continued in use. The Bible, however, like Cranmer's *Book of Common Prayer*, was published for the first time in the vernacular. Sweeping though these reforms were, they failed to satisfy those who were determined to 'purify' further the Church of England. These Puritans aimed to sup-

press any semblance of pomp in vestments and buildings and to concentrate on preaching from the Bible; some of them came to advocate the replacement of bishops with a presbyterian system of church government. There were Catholic subjects too who had no option but to accept the status quo and to pay fines for not attending church, sometimes practising the Mass secretly at home. The position of the Catholics worsened when Elizabeth felt threatened by possible support for her cousin and heir-apparent Mary Queen of Scots, whom she held in custody in England. A papal Bull of 1570 declaring Elizabeth to be a heretic provoked a crisis by seeming to give support to those Catholics who might have wished to put Mary on the throne. For almost twenty years the imprisoned fugitive Mary Stuart became a thorn in the flesh of Elizabeth, who was torn between fear of Catholic conspiracy and her sense of loyalty to another monarch, who was also a blood relative. Reluctantly, Elizabeth ordered Mary's execution in 1587, so that it was Mary's son James who was left to succeed the last of the Tudors.

**Fig. 10. MEDAL OF MARY I by Jacopo Trezzo, 1555.** This modern re-strike, in bronze, of a magnificent gold coin by Trezzo displays on the obverse a half-length figure of Mary from a portrait painted by Anthonis Mor. The Queen wears a jewel, probably one sent to her by her husband Philip of Spain, who may also have ordered the striking of the medal to commend Mary upon her government of the Kingdom

# EXPLORATION

Insular isolation has always determined England's dependence on trade with countries overseas. Accordingly, merchant ships and the men to sail them were commonplace around her coasts even in the Middle Ages, but it was in the sixteenth century that the seeds were sown which were to make England a great seapower. The declared aims of early explorers may have included the conversion of the heathen and a thirst for scientific knowledge, but the paramount goal was undoubtedly a search for wealth, which was to be acquired through trade or plunder. Earlier overland travellers had brought tales of the fabulous riches of the East, while Italian cities like Genoa and Venice acted as conduits for some of the goods that eventually filtered through to Britain. Most desired were spices such as pepper, nutmeg, cloves, cinnamon and ginger, very necessary to enhance the flavours of bland and often bad meat. Other luxuries attractive to merchants were fine silks and rare porcelains as well as gold which, it was believed, would be found in plenty.

The route to China (Cathay) and the Spice Islands by sea was already being explored by the Portuguese and Spanish. The Portuguese extended their knowledge of the African coast to find a route eastwards round the Cape of Good Hope whilst the Spanish chose the western course leading ultimately to the West Indies and the Americas. Pope Alexander VI, in order to prevent hostilities between these two countries, had initiated a treaty in 1494 which gave each of them rights to explore on one side or the other of an arbitrary line: south of the Azores the world was to be divided between them, east and west; the remaining European countries were ignored. So when Henry VII granted a charter to a group of Bristol merchants in 1497, the projected north-west route to China was a judicious choice. John Cabot headed the venture and set sail from Bristol to reach the north-east coast of America, probably Newfoundland (though he believed it was the coast of China). Cabot never

Fig. 11. TRADE DOLLAR, 1600. This large silver coin, modelled on the Spanish dollar, was issued for use in the East Indies in anticipation of the launch of the East India Company.

returned from a second voyage, undertaken in 1498; but by 1502 the New Foundland Company was formed, its main profit coming from fish.

During the reign of Henry VIII interest in adventurous exploration waned, partly because merchants were prospering in secure European markets and also because the King did not wish to antagonize the Spanish, with whom he had an alliance. It was during this reign, however that England prepared for her future power at sea. In the mid-sixteenth century, with the cloth trade in decline, the search for new markets initiated more exploration. Sailing again to the north in the search for a route to China, an expedition landed this time in Russia and in 1555 the Muscovy Company was officially given a monopoly of all trade and discovery in the north. This opened up new markets for English cloth and in return brought from Russia rope, flax, timber and wax (or tallow) for candles – a necessary commodity to lighten the gloom of Tudor houses.

**Fig.12. JOHN DEE. Portrait by an unknown British artist, painted between 1574 and 1586. A mathematician, astronomer, geographer and expert in navigation, Dee had great influence at court and in the development of navigation.**

Although the North-east passage to Asia proved elusive, the position of the British Isles on the edge of the Atlantic – the sea-route, it was hoped, to unimagined riches – was turned to advantage.

Exploration began in earnest in the reign of Elizabeth, when a few adventurers risked the wrath of the Spanish by trading along the coast of West Africa and even as far as the West Indies. The English geographer Richard Hakluyt (1552–1616), gives an account of many of the early voyages in his *Principal Navigations, Voyages and Discoveries of the English Nation* (1598–1600). Hakluyt himself did not travel to the New World but aimed to inspire his countrymen to greater achievement in the fields of exploration and settlement. He sought out first-hand information from sea-captains when they reached their home ports, documenting their experiences in a systematic manner that would benefit those who followed in the great adventure across the Atlantic. Another Elizabethan, John Dee

(1527–1608), though best remembered as an astrologer and alchemist, had a wide knowledge of navigation, mathematics and geography and was concerned for most of his life with the search for the elusive Northwest Passage to the Far East. Dee was the first man to use the expression 'British Empire', believing that Britain had rights over North America because a legendary Welsh prince, Owen Madoc, had founded colonies there in the twelfth century. Both Hakluyt and Dee promoted the idea of colonization in America, seeing it as potentially a rich source of raw materials and produce and alternatively as a market for industrial goods made in England.

Sir Walter Raleigh (1552–1618), courtier, navigator and author, was the promoter of many expeditions but most memorably of that which led to the first English settlement in America, giving it the name of Virginia in honour of Queen Elizabeth. However it was Sir Richard Grenville who set sail as head of that venture, for Elizabeth insisted that Raleigh remained in England. Accompanying the expedition of 1585 to Virginia were two men whose abilities were such that we have been left with an invaluable legacy in their work. The first was Thomas Hariot (1560–1621), a true Renaissance man whose curiosity about the natural world was equalled by his study of mathematics and science and whose navigational prowess was to be of prime importance to the future of exploration. Hariot lists the natural resources found in the colony, including pearls, grapes, fur, skins, iron, flax, hemp, pitch, cedar-wood and tobacco. The second of these outstanding figures was John White, a surveyor and an accurate draughtsman. White's maps and his drawings of the settlement showing the people and flora and fauna are of extraordinary value as the only pictorial record of the expedition. The first Virginian colony, on Roanoke Island, was intended to be not only a trading depot but also a convenient base for English ships to raid the Spanish West Indies or to harry Spanish ships. Privateering was a form of legalized piracy, some of the booty going to the Queen when ships docked in English harbours loaded with goods and precious

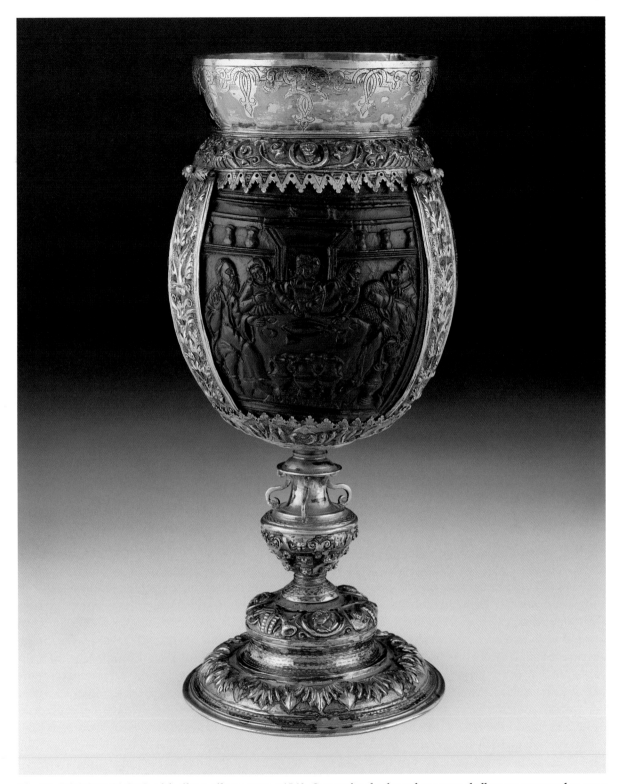

**Fig. 13. COCONUT CUP with silver-gilt mounts,** *c.*1560. Conveniently shaped coconut shells were mounted as cups by goldsmiths on account of their exoticism and suitability for decorative carving. The biblical scenes on this cup represent the Marriage at Cana, the Supper at Emmaeus, and Lot and his Daughters.

**Fig. 14. IZNIK JUG with silver-gilt mounts, London, 1586; maker's mark *IH*. Pottery from Iznik (Turkey) with its vivid palette, first appeared in England late in the sixteenth century. The quality of the silver mounts, with an engraved frieze of birds around the lip, reflects the prestige accorded to these exotic vessels.**

metals. The Roanoke settlement failed after only one year, with a few of the colonists returning home and the remainder perishing. Nevertheless England had a surplus of people eager to make the journey to new lands and to whom those territories not already occupied by Spain were very tempting. In the following century, many settlers were to follow in the wake of those first adventurers.

One English navigator who was called upon to help the first settlers in Virginia to make their journey home in 1586 was Francis Drake, one of Queen Elizabeth's most successful privateers. Some years earlier, in 1577, Drake had set sail to find a way to the East in command of an expedition of three ships. He intended to ignore Spanish suscepti-

bilities and to sail around Spanish South America, plundering as he went. The long journey was beset with difficulties and eventually only one of the ships crossed the Pacific. That ship was the *Golden Hind* and in it Drake eventually reached the Spice Islands, where he took on tons of cloves. After a voyage of thirty-three months, Drake arrived back in Plymouth to a hero's welcome and a knighthood from the Queen. As well as familiar spices and new types of food, treasure was brought back from the expedition. Drake brought a coconut for the Queen, who had its shell made into a decorative goblet. His stock at court must already have been high, but it is as the victor of a later sea-battle that Drake is best remembered.

# SHIPS AND GUNS FROM THE *MARY ROSE* TO THE ARMADA

In the expanding world of the sixteenth century the need for a well-ordered navy and efficient ships became paramount. Henry VII had encouraged and patronized explorers such as Cabot but in the fifteenth and sixteenth centuries most expeditions and the ships to sail them were privately funded. Larger ships owned by the Crown were hired out as merchant vessels in time of peace but could be recommissioned in case of war. At this time such ships remained little more than troop carriers, allowing soldiers to be taken to fight on land or to engage the enemy in hand-to-hand fighting at sea. The small naval inheritance left to his son by Henry VII consisted of five ships and one dockyard. Those ships would have had limited armaments, with small-calibre guns carried high up in the bow of the ship or in the stern castle.

Henry VIII's desire to have control of the seas around Britain was driven by economic as well as military considerations. England was heavily dependent for her wealth on the wool trade, which in turn required safe passage for the merchant vessels that provided a vital outlet to the European mainland. So it was that the typical vessels of the mid-fifteenth century were revolutionized into purpose-built men-of-war. By adding heavy cannon to their armoury the ships were invested with formidable power and a royal navy of professional seamen was founded. This was a disciplined organization that in the future would be capable of rebuffing the armadas of France and Spain and of securing the havens from which England's overseas adventures could be launched. Existing coastal defences were restored and a chain of forts was built along the shoreline of the south of England near Portsmouth and the Isle of Wight. In order to defend his forts and his ships Henry VIII had to bring about rapid improvement in the art of gunfounding in England. He was influenced by Scotland where there were already two of the most

advanced cannon foundries, established by his brother-in-law James IV. Technical experts were brought from overseas and guns too were imported. Henry VIII took a personal interest in the new technology and armaments of ships and saw his new ships as symbols of Tudor power.

At first the expansion of the navy was paid for by the monies received from the sale of monastic lands and when this was exhausted ships continued to be built or re-fitted to take account of the weight of the new armaments. It was recognized that stability would be compromised by merely adding heavier armaments in the former positions, so that new guns were re-sited on the lower decks, requiring ships to be built that would allow gunports to be placed close to the waterline and to be securely closed when not in use.

The *Mary Rose* was such a ship. Originally built in 1509 and named after Henry's favourite sister, the ship took part in many campaigns before being

Fig. 15. ADMIRALTY SEAL. The typical vessels of the mid-fifteenth century shown on the seal of the Admiral of England, Ireland and Aquitaine (1447-61) were revolutionized under Henry VIII into purpose-built men-of-war.

**Fig. 16. GOLD RYAL, 1584-5, worth 15 shillings or half a sovereign at this period. It shows Queen Elizabeth holding the orb and sceptre and standing in a galleon decorated with a Tudor rose.**

refitted in 1536. The *Mary Rose,* once refitted, was one of the first English warships that could be deployed as a tactical fighting unit. She sank in dramatic manner during an encounter with the French in the Solent in 1545, whilst Henry watched from the shore. The most likely cause for her sinking was that, when turning about, with the gunports open, the sea poured in causing the ship to capsize. Since her recovery in the 1980s from the sea-bed, along with many hundreds of artefacts, the *Mary Rose* has provided a complete inventory of the ordnance in use in 1545. Included were innovative cast bronze muzzle-loading guns carried low down as well as older, wrought-iron guns. In spite of the loss of the *Mary Rose,* Henry, who had begun his reign with a tiny complement of ships and armaments, by the time of his death had nearly sixty ships, three main dockyards and the first dry dock in the world.

The brief reigns of Edward VI and his sister Mary brought little change in tactics at sea. Indeed Mary, with her overwhelming sympathy towards the country of her mother and husband, wished England to be more dependent on the protection of the Spanish fleet. For the first twenty years of Elizabeth's reign too there was little improvement of the home fleet. The danger from France had been

removed and the rule of Philip II of Spain was at first marked by friendly intentions towards England. As the situation altered, a stronger navy was required and a number of corrupt or incompetent officials already in office were replaced. John Hawkyns was appointed Treasurer of the Navy; he was an experienced and practical sailor who now turned his talents to advising on naval matters. Unlike Henry VIII, Hawkyns saw little future in building large, heavily armed ships, since most sea battles continued to be fought on traditional lines with ships engaging each other close to the shore. His plan was to build an ocean-going fleet that could intercept supply routes to Spain. By cutting the source of Spain's wealth – gold and silver from America – Philip's forces would be made to suffer. In place of the out-of-date heavy ships he had built fast-sailing and manoeuverable fighting vessels that relied on expert seamanship and accurate firepower. The outcome was that by the time Hawkyns retired in 1587, the navy could muster over forty ships, all of them eminently seaworthy and representing a formidable fighting force.

Now rebuilt and renewed, the Queen's navy was ready and waiting for the invasion by Spain, a threat which had been rumoured abroad. Sir

**Fig. 17. ARMADA MEDAL, 1588. The obverse shows the Spanish fleet dispersed and wrecked, while above, in clouds is the name of Jehovah in Hebrew and the legend *FLAVIT. ET. DISSIPATI.SUNT.***

**Fig. 18. MODEL SHIP.** Formerly identified as Drake's *Golden Hind*, the model is now thought to represent a vessel built shortly after the death of Queen Elizabeth; nevertheless it gives a good impression of the appearance of an armed merchant ship at the end of her reign.

Francis Drake, in charge of one squadron of the fleet, had already covered himself in glory with his attack in 1587 on the Spanish ships while still in the safe haven of Cadiz harbour. In spite of this setback, the Spanish fleet reformed and the armada when it eventually set sail was formidable. Drake took steps to intercept the Spaniards before they could reach England but the winds were un-favourable, a situation that turned to the good fortune of the English. The Spanish were defeated by better ships, better seamanship, and to some extent the winds. The medal struck to commemo-rate the defeat of the Armada is inscribed *FLAVIT ET DISSIPATI SUNT* – 'He [i.e. God] blew and

they were scattered'– not the first time nor the last that success has been attributed to God being on the side of the victor.

With the defeat of the armada, Elizabeth still feared for the safety of England and her fears proved well founded, for the war with Spain continued. Nevertheless, the great victory was one based on new-style ships, superior skill and advanced tactics as well as luck. England now had a fleet that could acquit itself in any conflict; once a largely passive and defensive force, it was now poised to launch itself on the world stage in a manner that was to have profound consequences for England's economic and political development for centuries to come.

# ARCHITECTURE, ART, MUSIC AND LITERATURE

As demand for defensive and ecclesiastical projects slackened, masons in the Tudor period increasingly turned their skills to erecting well-appointed and comfortable houses. There was some ecclesiastical building in the early period, notably King's College Chapel, in Cambridge, built in the Late Perpendicular style, begun by Henry VI but not completed until the reign of Henry VIII. Mansions were designed on the traditional gothic plan, with the great hall forming the principal room of the house. Whilst the hall retained its importance as the first room of entry, it diminished in size and was supplemented with more retiring rooms, greater in size and number than formerly, so affording the family greater privacy and personal comfort. Brick became more popular and as glass became cheaper windows became larger and more plentiful.

There were as yet no professional architects but a master mason would plan a house, embellish and add to it later as required by the owner. This happened when Henry VIII acquired Hampton Court: wings and courtyards were added to include a tennis court, bowling alley and tiltyard, while heraldic insignia were applied to the towers and ceilings. For the ordinary householder, an original medieval structure might be extended by adding wings, resulting in a more imposing house. Clusters of long chimneys sprouted from the roofs, proclaiming the presence of numerous fireplaces, now invariably placed in the walls and not centrally. Diamond-shaped panes set in lead appeared in windows, allowing more light into rooms; nevertheless, interiors were still fairly dark and probably required candle-light on winter days as well as at night-time. In the lower levels of society and in the towns, timber-framed houses multiplied, the wall now filled out with brick rather than wattle-and-daub. The universal treatment applied to interiors was for the wood-panelling and for the furniture to be of oak; the latter was both functional and simple, though becoming increasingly heavily carved by the reign of Queen Elizabeth. At that time too the rooms were given added comfort with the addition of tapestries and other textiles. Rugs newly imported

**Fig. 19. HAMPTON COURT. Topographical view by Anthonis van den Wyngaerde. A contemporary view in watercolour with pen and ink.**

from Turkey were particularly sumptuous and were used to cover tables rather than the floor.

The patronage of the Tudor Court influenced painting as well as architecture. The first master-painters of the post-medieval period bequeathed to the country the rich legacy of portrait painting. Hans Holbein, a German who had spent time in Switzerland where he painted the portrait of Erasmus, worked at the court of Henry VIII and for the first time the likeness on canvas attempted to mirror the soul of the sitter as well as capture physical features. Elizabethan painters concentrated more on detailed representation of dress, jewellery and accessories, emphasizing the status of the sitter, sometimes in miniature. This particular style of painting grew out of manuscript illumination and was very much an English tradition. Nicholas Hilliard, the greatest of these miniaturists or limners, captured the age of Queen Elizabeth, painting exquisite, jewel-like portraits of the Queen and her courtiers. Trained as a goldsmith, Hilliard was also called upon to design and engrave Queen Elizabeth's second Great Seal.

Music, always the most widely accessible of the arts, had a rich inheritance from the medieval period in the songs that were sung both inside and outside church and the sixteenth century seems to have produced a burgeoning of musical talent. Both Henry VIII and Elizabeth were serious and talented musicians. On his death an inventory showed that in Henry VIII's household were 381 instruments,

Fig. 20. MINIATURE of an unknown man by Nicholas Hilliard, *c*.1590. Hilliard, 'limner and goldsmith' to Queen Elizabeth and James I was one of the finest miniaturists of all time and a leading light of the English Renaissance. The colours here, painted on card, have faded and there is a general air of dilapidation but the ghost of a great portrait still remains.

twenty-three of them guitars. However, simple pipes, drums or bells would have been the instruments available to ordinary folk. Viols and harpsichords were among the most popular at court, the former in its treble, tenor and bass forms suitable for playing in consort whilst the latter was mainly a

Fig. 21. TAPESTRY VALENCE, *c.*1580-1600. The design shows an allegorical scene, including in the background an Elizabethan knot garden. Sewn on linen with canvas support, it is embroidered with wool and silk threads, in tent, satin, running, laid couched, knot and stem stitches.

solo instrument. The violin had developed by the end of the sixteenth century but was not well known in England until much later when it came to eclipse the viol. Dancing, always a popular pastime, was particularly favoured at court and it was from here too that patronage of musicians writing for masques arose. Instrumental music, singing and dancing were important too in the drama, which saw a spectacular development at this time, and it is that art which has come to be particularly identified with the Elizabethan age.

Towards the end of Queen Elizabeth's reign William Shakespeare came to London, some time around 1592. Shakespeare was a stockholder and actor in the company named the Lord Chamberlain's Men, for whom he wrote an average of two plays a year. He was by no means the only great writer of his time: Ben Jonson, Christopher Marlowe and Edmund Spenser, to name but a few, were contemporaries, but Shakespeare's reputation stands head and shoulders above them all. Unlike anything that had gone before, the English language was used by these writers in a free and inventive way and most of all by Shakespeare. His imagery and dramatic vocabulary created effects never before experienced by audiences. Shakespeare, born in Stratford-upon-Avon in 1564 had a good education at the local grammar school. This involved a thorough grounding in Latin that stood him in good stead when he used his knowledge of classical history later in his writing. However his plays are alive with the characters he knew and grew up with in

Fig. 22. BASS VIOL, attributed to John Rose of Bridewell, London, *c.*1600, painted with the arms of Sir Charles Somerset (*c.*1585–1665), a member of the Beaufort family. The ornate body outline and other features are characteristic of the work of Rose (or Ross), one of the most famous makers at a time when English viol makers were the best in Europe.

**Fig. 23. BUST OF HENRY VIII.** Formerly in the collection of the Earl of Arundel the image was ultimately derived from medallic portraits which were in turn based on paintings or drawings.

Warwickshire and it is to that countryside that he turns for his most effective descriptions of nature, whether they be supposedly in Athens or Illyria! This too was the period of the new theatres. The troupes of players travelling from place to place – as those described in *Hamlet* – were now finding a home in purpose-built theatres like the *Globe* on the south bank of the Thames. In 1599, Shakespeare and six members of his group became owners of the *Globe*. Acting companies still travelled though, appearing frequently at court and escaping to the country when the plague invaded the city. Shakespeare's plays were not published in definitive form during his lifetime; because each actor would be given only his own part there was no requirement to produce a complete text. Shakespeare and some of the other writers of the period lived on into the Stuart age, but it was the age of Elizabeth that nurtured their talent. The Renaissance in the arts in Elizabethan England may not have equalled that of some European countries in terms of architecture and painting, but nowhere did literature achieve such heights.

Fig. 24. WEDDING CUP. Design for a gold cup set with jewels, by Hans Holbein. The cup was made for Henry VIII *c.*1536-7, in commemoration of the King's marriage to Jane Seymour on 30 May 1536 (Jane was to die the following year). The cover bears the inscription *BOUND TO OBEY AND [SERVE]*. The initials *H & J* are repeated at intervals.

# SOCIAL CHANGE

Society in Tudor England remained highly status-conscious: from the monarch and the aristocracy, by way of the gentlemen and yeomen to the lowest levels in society – everyone knew their place. Within this highly structured hierarchy, however, there was a degree of mobility that saw the fortunes of some rise while others fell. This was an era of change with new opportunities for advancement, especially by way of growing bureaucracies and new professions as well as through the expansion in trade which brought wealth to those who had not had it in former times. For those intent on climbing the social ladder there were advantages to keeping company with those of higher rank and even more so if an advantageous marriage could be engineered.

Evidence of a step-up in society would be flaunted in a number of ways, most obviously in one's outward appearance but also more formally in the right to bear arms. In order for a family to confirm that it had wealth and position it was necessary to show it and generous hospitality was a particularly effective way of doing so. Not only was superior status displayed by way of the expense lavished on tableware but also through the kinds of food provided and in the method of its presentation.

In the upper echelons of society dining habits altered, in part due to changes in dwelling houses. Once the communal medieval hall had been replaced by a variety of smaller rooms, dining became a more private affair for the owner and his

**Fig. 25. TRENCHERS, placed face-down on the dinner table, served as platters from which fruit could be eaten. Following the meal they were turned over and the rhymes and sayings inscribed on them were used in after-dinner games. This square set with specially made box shows regular script and delicate details; probably it dates from the early years of Elizabeth's reign.**

family. There would still be formal occasions when large numbers of people dined in the great hall but, on the whole, gone were the days when the entire household sat down together to eat.

The buffet or court cupboard, a new piece of furniture, appeared in the dining room specifically to store and display the family silver or other precious vessels. If the guests could eat from a table laden with silver objects and still leave the buffet displaying a surplus, so much the better. Even this would be beyond the pocket of the great majority of the population and it was only the aristocrats, the merchants and professional classes who aspired to owning elaborate tableware. In times of need the silver tableware could be melted down and converted into cash: much early silver is lost to us because of this practice. Succeeding generations also preferred to own the latest styles and so the inherited silver would be changed periodically for the prevailing fashion. With the exception of the silver plate available to the wealthiest members of society, dishes and platters were normally made of pewter or wood. English pottery vessels and dishes were very basic and were kept as useful kitchen equipment in upper-class homes. More elegant wares that provided evidence of rank were imported, such as Venetian glass, ceramics in the form of maiolica from Italy and Iznik wares from Turkey. Precious ceramics and glass were sometimes mounted with silver-gilt fittings as were the finer wooden bowls known as mazers.

Cutlery was not provided by the host: guests were expected to bring their own knife and spoon. Silver spoons were frequently given as christening presents and their survival in fairly large numbers may owe something to the fact that they were passed on in bequests. For poorer folk, again pewter provided a substitute. Forks were available for cooking but were not yet commonly in use in England at the table, although it is said that Queen Elizabeth was given one. First used in Italy, forks were small, usually with two prongs and were not meant to be put into the mouth but rather to spear sticky sweetmeats that would then be transferred to the fingers. Sweetmeats or conceits were served at the end of a meal, presented on wooden roundels or trenchers.

**Fig. 26. SILVER SPOON, 1520, with the figure of St. James the Less holding a fuller's bat, the instrument of his martyrdom. London was the dominant centre for goldsmith's work in the period and several London workshops made a speciality of spoon-making. Sets of Apostle spoons, with the finial formed as Christ or one of the Apostles identified by their emblems were much favoured in Tudor and early Stuart England.**

These trenchers were frequently ornamented on one side with an intricate design of fruit, flowers, leaves or nuts with interwoven strapwork encircling a rhyming stanza of doggerel which might form the basis of after-dinner games. Sugar had become more plentiful, allowing elaborate confections to be made.

Marzipan and dried fruits would also have been enjoyed from fruit trenchers.

The rich had access to more sugary foods and meat than was good for them, added to which they did not eat enough fresh vegetables and fruit; their diet was, by today's standards, highly unbalanced. Salt was used in great quantities both in cooking and for preserving as a means of making food more palatable. All of these factors contributed to widespread ill health and bad teeth. Exploration to other lands introduced more supplies of new and exotic foods that were a boon to cooks, who began to make rich stews which included fruits and spices, helping to disguise meat which might have gone off. Most Tudor food, whether fish or meat was served in, or with, sauces flavoured with herbs and spices. When meat was available it was frequently boiled in a large metal pot suspended above the fire or spit-roasted on a turn-spit with the fat being collected beneath and re-used for lighting. It was during the Tudor period that the method of cooking over charcoal-burning stoves developed. This system, for which pottery pipkins and skillets were used, allowed the cooks to prepare more delicate dishes and sauces in smaller quantities. Chafing dishes were introduced to keep food warm or to prepare small amounts away from the main stoves or fire.

**Fig. 27. LEATHER COSTREL of the sixteenth century Costrels were made by soaking the leather and moulding it over a wooden former; decoration was also applied while the leather remained wet. When sewn together and thoroughly dried, costrels made strong, light-weight vessels ideal for the traveller. A bottle of this size would have been carried strapped to the saddle. Included in the original ornament here are two devices – a pomegranate and a Tudor rose – the one alluding to Catherine of Aragon and the other to Henry VIII.**

**Fig. 28. SKILLET** with green glaze and hollow handle that probably had a wooden extension for grasping. This shallow tripod pot was a new type of cookware. Its small size gives an indication of the more refined form of food preparation which began to take place at this time.

As it had been in the medieval period, religion was an important factor in Tudor eating habits. Meat was not eaten on Fridays, never eaten during the forty days of Lent and, for some, restricted on other days too. Fish therefore became an important part of the menu. Both freshwater and saltwater fish were eaten. Freshwater species like carp, bream and trout came from local rivers, while the monarch and the nobility would have access to their own fishponds or a moat.

It was a different story for the poor; for them meat was a rarity, except for what could be caught in the wild – and this was highly restricted. Unless they lived near the sea, fresh fish would also be a luxury and of course all food was dependent on the season. The Tudor housewife became adept at preserving what she could, so that the larder would not be empty through the long winter. Very important was the organization of the dairy, butter and cheese being a vital source of protein. This was one reason why milk was not drunk in larger quantities, for it was required for making these

essentials; another reason was that cows yielded much less milk in the sixteenth century than they do today. Bread was of course an important part of everyone's diet, but even the type of bread you ate reflected your status in society.

Water was little drunk as it was widely considered unsafe and it was beer or ale that was consumed by most people. Ale was the weaker substance whilst beer had the added benefit of hops, which gave it longer-lasting qualities. Vast quantities of wine were consumed by the court and nobility, but all of it had to be imported since the practice of growing vines in England had died out by the sixteenth century.

It was in Tudor England that, along with an accumulation of new types of food and more efficient methods of cooking and preserving, there came a proliferation of books on the subject of etiquette and 'receipts'. How one presented a table to one's guest was of great consequence, as were the rituals of hygiene associated with eating – a very different picture from that commonly held.

# THE COUNTRYSIDE

Throughout the Tudor period, England remained overwhelmingly rural in character: the population has been estimated at perhaps 2.5 – 3 million souls, sharing the country with some 8 million sheep. None the less, far-reaching changes were registered in the course of the sixteenth century. The dissolution of the monasteries saw ownership of vast estates transferred initially to the Crown but subsequently redistributed in an extended process of sales, gifts and exchanges: over half the estates were alienated by the end of Henry VIII's reign and by the accession of Elizabeth the proportion had risen to three-quarters. Land prices were stimulated by this redistribution of ownership and had doubled in value by 1600.

At the beginning of the sixteenth century much of the landscape remained covered with hardwood forest which, for all that it supplied the meagre populace with the bulk of its fuel and building materials, remained largely intact. A number of industries such as tanning and charcoal-burning were supported here, while coppicing was extensively practised. Open woodlands and the strays with which they were interspersed provided grazing for large numbers of pigs as well as cattle and horses.

Horses represented a major and indispensable resource without which the rural economy would have collapsed. Henry VIII, aware of their strategic as well as their economic value, introduced legislation that aimed to improve the quality of the national stock by banning under-sized animals from common grazing, while new blood was constantly being

**Fig. 29. HORSES were required in large numbers when a long journey was undertaken by members of the Court, regular changes of the animals being necessary en route. The illustration shows Cardinal Wolsey riding to London on his way to France.**

**Fig. 30. LONDON BRIDGE _c._1575–90. The river is shown busy with traffic and the bridge lined with buildings.**

added in the form of imports from Ireland, from the continental mainland as far away as Spain and Italy, and from the Near East. Saddle-horses were perpetually in demand and with the introduction of the coach during the reign of Elizabeth came an additional need for well-matched teams of animals. Traction on the farm was provided in some areas primarily by horses and in others by oxen. In addition to carts and wagons there were ploughs to be hauled, varying from heavy, double-wheeled varieties (often communally owned) in some areas to somewhat flimsy foot-ploughs in others.

An increasing awareness of the potential for improvement of arable land can be detected as the century progresses, reflected in the publication of growing numbers of published tracts that counselled

31

the landowner in the adoption of one regime or another. Some inroads were made into the rather fatalistic attitude that coloured national attitudes to the land – that its topography, soil and other natural characteristics fundamentally conditioned what might be expected of it. As the possibilities for improvement by more intensive fertilization and by rudimentary rotation of crops were grasped, yields on existing arable land were improved, more pasture came under the plough and forest clearance gathered pace. While the open fields of the south midlands maintained their character during this period, large areas of the south-east (as well as the south-west and the west midlands) were progressively enclosed with hedges. Wheat, rye, barley and oats formed the principal grain crops, with beans and peas accounting for the bulk of the remainder. Fruit-growing expanded markedly in the south-east and hops were introduced to this area from the Continent; market-gardening grew up around London, some of it in the hands of Netherlandish immigrants. Hemp and flax were widely grown in small plots and in some areas (notably the Fens) formed a major element of the local economy.

Far more striking than the extent of the arable land, however, was the proportion of the countryside given over to pasture. Foreign visitors (for whom the amount of land under the plough provided the principal index of success) were invariably rather dismissive of English agriculture, but they were universally impressed by the numbers and the quality of animals reared in the countryside and by the correspondingly high-protein diet enjoyed by a large part of the populace. Beef and mutton in particular were widely available, as were milk and cheese. A large part of the cereal and leguminous crop production mentioned above was earmarked for fodder; a great deal of it, furthermore, was produced for purely local consumption, placing an effective limit on the potential for population growth in the major county towns such as York, Coventry, Salisbury and Bristol, and even in London itself (far greater in size, but with a population estimated at only 60-70,000). A multiplicity of breeds could be found in the livestock populations of the various regions, some of which gradually became specialized either in breeding animals or in fattening them for the market, according to the topography and natural resources of the area.

The road network was of very indifferent quality, and although it was possible – with a relay of post-horses stationed along the route – to make the journey from Edinburgh to London in the space of a few days, in practice life moved at a more leisurely pace. Wherever possible, the road system followed the hard soils provided by elevated ground, but where it had to cross marshy or flood-prone areas, causeways might be built. The roads were thronged not only with horse transport (mostly pack-horses and saddle-horses, for carts and wagons still found the going difficult) but also, because of the enclosure of land, with numbers of unemployed vagrants who wandered the countryside, to the consternation of those in authority.

Given the generally poor condition of the roads, waterways were used whenever possible. Situated on navigable rivers, towns like York, Gloucester, Norwich and Oxford could be described as inland ports. The populace of London used the Thames as the most wholesome means of communication in preference to the malodorous and fetid streets of the capital and, with London Bridge as the only direct crossing point, the river traffic was intense. 'Thames wherries' were the most common type of craft used for carrying passengers and through an Act of 1555 the Watermen's Company was born. Later Queen Elizabeth granted arms to the Company and the Watermen were the first public servants to wear a uniform. As well as its importance for commercial purposes, the River Thames formed a backdrop for much pomp and pageantry in Tudor times, as when the City livery companies decked out their barges to follow that of the Lord Mayor on the occasion of his annual procession (an event which resorted to land only in the nineteenth century).

Coastal towns found the sea route the obvious choice for intercommunication, as well as for the long-distance carriage of heavy goods. The coalfields of the north-east for example transported large

Fig. 31. ARMORIAL DELFTWARE MUG. This early eighteenth-century example of English Delftware pottery bears a fine study of the arms of the Company of Thames Watermen and Lightermen, granted by Queen Elizabeth in 1583. Henry VIII had earlier passed a statute regulating the fares which the watermen or wherrymen could levy and finally an Act of 1555 founded the Company.

quantities of coal from Newcastle to London to satisfy a growing demand during the sixteenth century.

As interest in the topography of Great Britain grew and a thirst for knowledge about the country needed to be satisfied, great advances in cartography were made by men such as Christopher Saxton and John Speed. For the first time maps were published which reproduced in a useful and purposeful manner the true disposition of the land, in contrast to the highly impressionistic representations of the medieval period.

# TUDOR LEARNING

From the primary school to university level, there was considerable expansion in education in the Tudor period. The instruction of the young was considered the responsibility of the mother until her charges reached the age of seven. After that there was the 'petty' school where basic literacy was taught; for some there was the further possibility of a pre-apprenticeship training which might include grounding in mathematics, accounting and similar practical skills. Later a master would be expected to teach his apprentice his craft and how to run a business. For those wishing to better themselves there was the grammar school, where the curriculum concentrated on Latin and Greek grammar. The son of a wealthy man might be taught at home by a tutor but there was also the possibility of attending one of the many public schools founded at this time. Girls were excluded from grammar schools and

universities and only those with a private tutor could expect to receive anything beyond basic reading and writing.

Education was inextricably bound to religion and, for some, a priest might be the family tutor and the local village school would often be placed in the care of the parish priest. After the break with Rome, schools linked to monasteries or chantries were frequently refounded as secular educational establishments when the Crown sold off the lands of their parent institutions. This is not to say that in secular schools religion did not play a large part in the education of children; for some parents enabling their children to read the Bible was sufficient reason for imparting to them the fundamentals of literacy.

In spite of the expansion in the provision of education, for the poorest in society the need for

**Fig. 32. APPRENTICE BOXES.** These onion-shaped money-boxes were traditionally used for Christmas savings by apprentices. The coins saved during the year could be retrieved only by breaking the box.

ELIZABETHA ANGLIÆ REGINA

By Gods great power being set in regall Throne,
I happily have ruld my state in peace,
My zeale to him, and subjects good alone,
Was my chiefe care; and willingly to ease
My neighbour countries: who were fore opprest
With bloudy wars, 'gainst them by Spaniards made,

I shewed my love to give their toiles some rest,
And spared nothing of the meanes I had.
I then Protectrix was of all that State,
And did defend them 'gainst the furious spight
Of Spanish forces, which could not amate
My resolution, whilest I breathd this light.

**Fig. 33. QUEEN ELIZABETH, engraving, 1592, by Crispin van der Passe. Elizabeth is said to be wearing the dress she wore to St. Paul's at the celebration of the defeat of the Spanish Armada. The expansion of printing in the sixteenth century allowed greatly increased access to images such as this.**

**Fig. 34. BRONZE MOUNT in the form of a hand holding a pen, sixteenth-century. It may once have ornamented a writing case.**

their young children to work and help support the family overrode any possibility of their taking advantage of the free grammar school.

The sixteenth and early seventeenth centuries saw a considerable movement in higher education too, not only through the expansion of facilities but also through a fundamental change in character. Education was extended from the purely theological training of priests and scholars to that which would, at the highest level, include the possibility for an accomplished gentleman to serve the state and if possible better himself in society. The medieval idea of a gentleman as one combining prowess in knightly tournaments with courtly manners was to be supplemented with classical learning and rhetorical skill. The clergy had always had a degree of schooling; now the gentry joined them in the desire to acquire the polish of a university education. New colleges were founded at Oxford and Cambridge and the Inns of Court too expanded to accommodate the growing numbers seeking a legal education - a very useful training if one wished to gain a position in politics or administration.

Running parallel to the growth in education came the desire for more books. Improvement in paper manufacture and the setting up of the first English printing press by William Caxton in 1476 helped to supply the growing demand. The printing and publishing trade not only provided information in book form and pamphlets but also stimulated demand for more knowledge, at the same time creating many new possibilities for skilled employment. New translations into English of the Bible and other religious tracts most probably dominated the output, but there were opportunities to popularize other subjects. Treatises on practical accomplishments like archery and cookery, surveys of the country and towns and map-making were among the growing list of printed works. We have already seen how the geographical works of John Dee and Richard Hakluyt provided information on the wider world.

While the years of great scientific discoveries lay in the future, advances were made in some disciplines. In medicine, for example, although the training was mainly theoretical and based on the writings of classical philosophers, practical observation was beginning to be valued, such as the examination of the patient's urine as a means of diagnosis. It was in the sixteenth century that the dissection of corpses and the proper study of anatomy began slowly to become part of a doctor's training. University-trained physicians comprised only a small percentage of those who practised medicine and the man-in-the-street probably turned more frequently to the apothecary or the barber-surgeon.

The description of the apothecary's shop in Shakespeare's *Romeo and Juliet* illustrates the combination of natural remedies and quasi-magical cures that were on offer.

*"I do remember an apothecary,…*
*And in his needy shop a tortoise hung,*
*An alligator stuff'd, and other skins*
*Of ill-shaped fishes; and about his shelves*
*A beggarly account of empty boxes,*
*Green earthen pots, bladders, and musty seeds,*
*Remnants of packthread, and old cakes or roses*
*Were thinly scattered, to make up show."*

Romeo and Juliet; Act V, Scene 1.

**Fig. 35. WATCH, 1580–1590, signed Francis Nawe at London. Nawe was a member of the Dutch Church in London, 1583.**

The study of astrology, an elaborate blend of mysticism and science, was a standard part of medical practice as well as being used for forecasting auspicious dates for important events. John Dee, astrologer to Queen Elizabeth, chose the most favourable day for her coronation. Another indication of the popularity of astrology can be seen in the growing publication of almanacs at this time.

Educational expansion gave more opportunities for knowledge to be turned to practical use. Navigators had found it difficult to establish their position at sea since they had no way of determining longitude. Efforts were made to develop accurate timekeepers, enabling sailors to carry the home-port time aboard ship so that they could calculate more accurately the distance they had travelled to east or west. The Flemish astronomer Gemma Frisius in 1530 was one of those who worked on this problem, but the clocks of the early sixteenth century were not equal to the task and its final resolution was to take a further two centuries.

The step that turned a portable clock into a watch (i.e. the change from weight suspension to a spring) was a practical one and early watch-makers were craftsmen rather than scholars. Until the late seventeenth century watches had only one hand and required constant winding. The earliest clocks and watches made in England in the second half of the sixteenth century were rare and on the whole were the work of immigrant craftsmen from Germany, the Netherlands or France.

Fig. 36. MEMORIAL BRASSES and tomb sculptures provide vivid and often detailed evidence for variations in dress. This inscised brass dating from *c*.1520, and probably originating in East Anglia, shows a middle-class lady in mob-cap and full-length gown, with a large rosary and a metal-framed purse hanging from her girdle.

# DRESS AND JEWELLERY

The tendency for new fashions to originate at Court before working their way down through society was as true in the Tudor period as in any other. New styles among the nobility and the upper classes were frequently introduced from abroad by visiting dignitaries (or even by their portraits, sent as gifts), from travellers' tales and the growth in supply of exotic materials. At the beginning of the sixteenth century the strongest influence came from Germany, favouring strong, bright colours and the use of sumptuous velvets, satins, furs and cloth of gold. After the succession of Mary Tudor in mid century, colourful and often ostentatious clothes gave way to the Spanish taste for wearing black. This fashion may have arisen from the introduction into Spain of a new dye that for once produced a truly deep black: extracted from the logwood tree, discovered by the Spanish in South America, this black dye being both new and expensive, was naturally associated with luxury, and hence with desirability. Extravagant ruffs replaced the soft collars of the early period (it was during the reign of Queen Elizabeth that starching was introduced) and the farthingale (a wooden framework beneath the skirt) emphasized (or at least suggested) a tiny waist. These features, together with a preference for more fitted styles, gave the wearer a more rigid and haughty look.

Costly materials and jewels may have been within the means of some prosperous merchants, doctors and lawyers, but the middle classes were forbidden such things because of sumptuary laws, which sought to control undue ostentation but which were often more honoured in the breach than the observance. However, many of these wealthy up-and-coming families had portraits painted of themselves and their families wearing the latest styles.

This was the period when clothes were slashed to reveal an undershirt or lining which was then pulled through the slits to form decorative pouches. It was a time of the codpiece, the stomacher, square-toed shoes and soft hats; everyone, other than those who worked manually, would have worn gloves. Embroidery was very popular and further enhanced the silks and satins studded with jewels, while pomanders hung from the waist to ward off evil smells.

The dress of poorer people changed very little. In any case, delicate fabrics, elaborate ornaments and the stiff supports worn by the wealthy would have been out of place in the workplace, even if such luxuries had been attainable. The practical and cheap garments of the lower classes were likely to be made of coarse linen or English wool.

In spite of limitations for the middle and lower classes, explorations and discoveries in the Elizabethan period increased the availability of beautiful

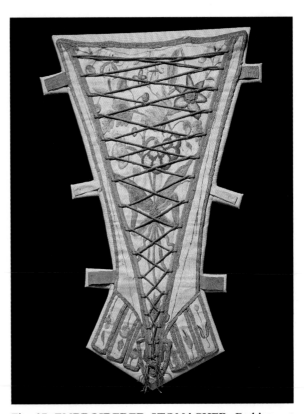

**Fig. 37. EMBROIDERED STOMACHER. Fashions at times became so extreme as to demand mechanical aids to mould the figure into the desired shape.**

Fig. 38. SHOES of white suede. The well-formed heels were an innovation of the 1590s. This pair can be dated to the turn of the century, when they would have represented the height of fashion.

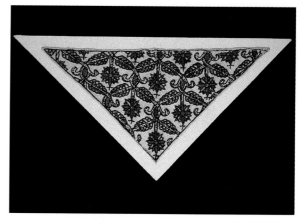

Fig. 39. FOREHEAD-CLOTH, embroidered with leaf and flower motif. The cloth formed a decorative peak to complement the head-dress.

Fig. 40. GLOVES, said to have been presented to Queen Elizabeth in 1566 when she visited Oxford. It was customary at that time to present royal visitors with at least a dozen pairs of gloves. This pair may have been made at Woodstock. Tradition has it that despite their fine craftsmanship, their unflatteringly large size may have caused the Queen to leave them behind.

fabrics, previously available to a limited number. Silks, satins, velvets and lace came from abroad along with precious and semi-precious stones that would be sewn on to garments or set into jewellery.

The evidence from royal portraits, if not from actual survival of the objects themselves, suggests that the Tudors loved jewellery to extremes. From hair-jewels and hat-badges down to decorated shoes, there seemed to be no part of the costume or body that could not be enhanced by the addition of jewellery. Jewels not only added lustre and richness to materials but also many of the pieces had a significance, either political or religious.

In spite of the Reformation, religious items were still worn, especially crosses, but after the reign of Mary Tudor rosaries were forbidden and recusant families had to wear them secretly, sometimes as rings. Also banned in the reign of Queen Elizabeth were items such as reliquaries that might contain a splinter from the True Cross or a scrap of material from a saint. Girdle prayer books gave goldsmiths the opportunity to show their skills as these tiny books would be bound in gold, enamelled and often encrusted with jewels. The influence of classical antiquity also ensured the renewed popularity of engraved gems. Cameos were popular and original Roman gems and coins were sometimes mounted and worn as jewellery. Those entitled to wear livery collars, chains, medals and Garter insignia made full use of the artistry of the goldsmith, enamelling being particularly favoured. Intricate knot designs and ciphers were popular Renaissance ornamental motifs often worked into jewellery. Watches were very poor timekeepers, but nevertheless could be a beautiful and elaborate addition to hang from the waist like a chatelaine, showing one to be in the forefront of new ideas.

Almost everyone could own a ring and they were put to many uses: even a man averse to any form of frippery might have a signet ring, a memorial or *memento mori* ring. One form was the English posy ring (the name deriving from poesy or poetry) which, although outwardly plain, was often engraved within the hoop with words of love. Many people wore charm or magical rings, as they had done in medieval times, for their prophylactic qualities; the toadstone was one that retained its popularity from those times. Portraits of the royal family show that they might wear many elaborate rings on a number of fingers.

Anything that could be worn to display status in society was turned into a beautiful object by the Tudor goldsmith and although only a fraction have survived they continue to gleam out at us from contemporary portraits.

**Fig. 41. MINIATURE of** *AN ELDERLY MAN IN A BLACK HAT,* **by Isaac Oliver. Painted on vellum inscribed in elegant gold letters,** *ANNO DOMINI 1588.* **The high-crowned hat was a Spanish fashion which probably came in during the reign of Queen Mary, but the flat bonnet type was never out of favour.**

**Fig. 42. THREE SIXTEENTH-CENTURY RINGS: a)** gold signet, the oval bezel engraved with the sacred monogram *IHS* in a true lovers' knot and the hoop chased with leaves on the shoulders; **b)** charm-ring with opposed bezels, each set with a toadstone, one of the most prized charm-stones; **c)** gold *memento mori* ring, with a hexagonal bezel inscribed *BEHOLD THE EN[D]* around a skull, providing the wearer with a constant reminder of his mortality.

41

# SPORTS AND PASTIMES

Familiarity with the arts and with natural and speculative philosophy was not enough to make a complete 'Renaissance man'; physical skills were considered as important in the making of a gentleman as the more cerebral pursuits. King Henry VIII was a supreme example of such a man; a composer of music and poetry and an able debater with scholars, he could yet claim to outdo all of his courtiers at dancing, hunting, jousting and drinking.

At the Field of Cloth of Gold, an extended series of celebrations and competitions between the French and English courts held near Guînes in the Pas-de-Calais in 1520, Henry and his courtiers were able to match their accomplishments against those of Francis I of France. Days filled with tournaments and jousting were followed by evenings of dancing and masques, no less competitive, in which the two monarchs took full part. On this occasion Tudor refinement and aristocratic prowess were put to their ultimate test and can be said to have survived the ordeal with some credit.

Outdoor pursuits were widely popular. The medieval sport of hawking continued to be popular and was one of the few in which ladies might take part. Hawking, not a favourite with Henry in his younger days, latterly suited him well and he built a mews to house his hawks at Greenwich Palace. A particular favourite with the nobility was the chase, involving deer-hunting on horseback. Hares and other game were also pursued, but there was little or no interest in foxhunting at this time. These sports required a degree of horsemanship from the participants, a skill which formed an essential part of the training of a man of culture. Horse and rider had to be graceful in movement as well as forceful: the names of several Italian riding masters appear in court records during Henry's reign and in the following decades, showing an eagerness to absorb the latest continental equestrian fashions.

Jousting skills were honed in competitive exercises involving 'running at the ring', in which the rider sought to penetrate a suspended hoop with

**Fig. 43. BORDER DETAIL from an engraved portrait of Henry VIII after an original by Holbein. The scene illustrates a tournament taking place at the Field of Cloth of Gold.**

the tip of his lance. Although Henry VIII was to give up jousting by 1530, probably because of the onset of middle age and the danger of injury, he continued to hunt until late in life. Horses were to be enjoyed as a spectator sport too and it was in 1530 that the first organized racing took place at York. At this period two-horse races were the norm.

The tournament involved hand-to-hand combat as well as jousting, but under the Tudors it evolved into a more formalized and dramatic presentation of courtly life in which elaborate pageantry and allegorical display began to outweigh the outright violence of medieval jousts. From its place in the tiltyard during the day, the sport became part of a range of indoor revels that included dancing and masques staged to accompany evening banquets.

Such amusements were beyond the reach of the lower orders but they could exercise their physical prowess in wrestling bouts and in archery competitions using the longbow. Recreational use of the crossbow was restricted to the nobility and gentry. Other spectator sports such as cock-fighting and bear- or bull-baiting were enjoyed by all ranks in society. Both Henry VIII and Queen Elizabeth had areas set aside within their palace precincts for such pastimes. Bowling alleys similarly provided for the monarch's recreation, and these were also to be found more widely dispersed in country seats and village inns where skittles as well as bowls were played.

Indoor sports provided less taxing forms of exercise. Tennis, a new game originating in France, was largely limited to the nobility, being played with rackets in a walled and roofed court. It was taken up with enthusiasm by Henry VIII, who built courts at all his major palaces.

Dancing was one of the most favoured indoor pastimes at court. Queen Elizabeth in particular was fond of showing off her dancing skills by performing the galliard and the volta before the assembled court. It was during the sixteenth century that the fashion for masques came to England from continental Europe: they became hugely popular at court, where elaborate costumes and spectacular scenery combined with rich allegorical verse provided new means for entertaining and flattering the monarch.

**Figs. 44–45. HENRY VIII'S HAWKING EQUIPMENT.** The hawk's hood (above) is of leather, to which is sewn a cover of red velvet; the cover is decorated with embroidery involving loops of gold, and is edged with gold chain-work. The glove, for the right-hand (below), is of reddish-brown doeskin with an overlaid panel of grey-white kid or dogskin on the upper palm; it is embroidered with rows of silver-gilt thread held by red silk couching stitches. The style and decoration are consistent with the type of embroidered glove worn in the early sixteenth century.

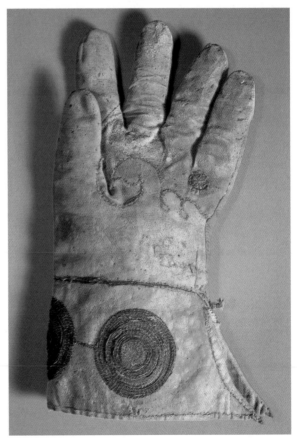

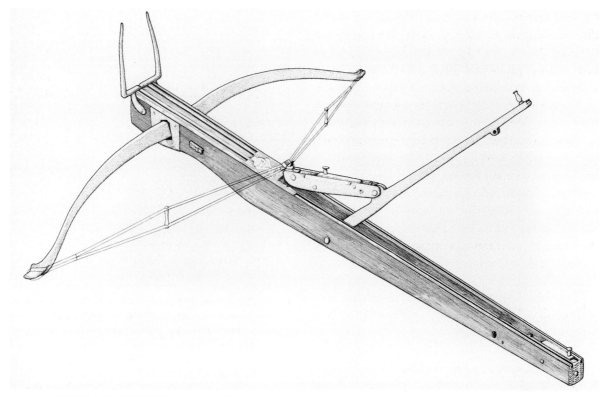

Fig. 46. STONE CROSSBOW, which differs from the ordinary crossbow in that it shoots not bolts but stone 'bullets'. Although popular for hunting from the later Middle Ages onwards, by the sixteenth century they were considered weapons fit for a king. Henry VIII had at least one stone crossbow in his possession at the time of his death.

The English considered themselves a musical nation. Not only was dancing popular but there were many amongst the educated classes who were accomplished singers with the ability to read music and sing in four-, six- or eight-part harmony. The fashionable Elizabethan lute was an expensive instrument; so too were the virginals, which the Queen could play. Viols and the recorder were popular and some barbers kept citterns (known as the poor man's lute) in their shops so that customers could play on them while they waited their turn to have their beard trimmed. Itinerant musicians such as fiddlers played for the general public, who also enjoyed theatrical performances. There were no permanent theatres outside London, but inns, village greens and market squares offered all that was needed for travelling players who, since medieval times, had gone about the country giving dramatic performances of well-known tales. It was a different matter altogether in the capital, for it was towards the end of the reign of Elizabeth that the first permanent theatres were being built with professional acting companies to perform in them.

Another legacy of the Tudor era, still in evidence today, is the game of cards, which became popular at this time, promoted by greater ease of availability due to the development of printing. The earliest cards had been hand-painted and those produced in England show the court cards as figures dressed in the style of Henry VII; traditionally it is thought that Henry's wife Elizabeth of York was the model for the Queen. The design of the pack remains largely unchanged to the present day.

The peasants worked long and hard and had to make the most of Sundays and holy days. Football, always popular among the youths, was very physical and boisterous, often causing injury, and unsuccessful attempts were made periodically to ban it. A new game known as 'crickette' is recorded in 1598 although a similar game played with bat and ball had certainly been known in medieval times; this sport became formalized only in the eighteenth century. For leisure hours indoors the poorer people could play shovel-board, nine men's morris and tables (a form of backgammon) in the local inn. Dice games were also popular, though frowned on by the Church. As an accompaniment to these leisure-time pursuits, a new habit introduced in 1588 was to find almost overnight favour: this was the smoking of tobacco, brought back from the New World and so rapidly adopted by society that by the time of Elizabeth's death there were already a substantial number of clay pipe makers to cater for the demand from inns and private households up and down the country.

Fig. 48. EMBROIDERED COIF OR CAP (detail) sewn with blackwork stitches and metal threads. The geometric and floral design includes rose, pomegranate and pea-pod motifs.

Fig. 47. CITTERN by Gasparo da Salò, Brescia, *c.*1560. The pegbox decorated with the carved head of a female figure wearing a ruff, has a hook at its back. There are eleven strings, grouped as four double courses and three single courses.

Whilst peasant women may have participated in country games on the village green, the remainder of their sex had to content themselves in public as spectators. The leisure time of privileged ladies was more characteristically spent with embroidery, a professional craft in medieval times but one which now gave women an opportunity to develop dexterity and artistic skill. The flowering of this new accomplishment climaxed in the final decades of the sixteenth century, at which time the added benefits of imported silk thread and improved steel needles made an impact. The English use of blackwork was particularly popular in decorating fine linen for clothes and other personal items. As a category of embroidery, blackwork, thought to have originated in Spain and probably ultimately derived from Arabic designs, became fashionable in England during the sixteenth century when Catherine of Aragon married Henry VIII. Traditionally done with black silk thread on white or cream linen, it consisted of repeated geometric patterns using a combination of basic embroidery stitches. The Elizabethans loved embroideries to have patterns that reflected the natural world around them: flowers, plants, nuts and berries were popular motifs. So it was that when this type of Spanish needlework became fashionable it took on a peculiarly English style, occasionally even being worked on gold or with red or gold thread instead of black. Other favourite devices for embroidery were heraldic emblems or badges and even knot gardens were represented, the latter combining a love of pattern with a love of nature. All or any of these could be used to enhance books, which might be bound with velvet then closely embroidered all over with gold thread and seed-pearls. In wealthier homes tapestries were prominent as hangings for the wall, as curtains or as valences for beds, and as cushions to give softness to plain wooden furniture. Although carpets were imported from Turkey and the Levant, they were also made by the English to their own taste.

**Fig. 49. TRAVELLING GAME-BOARD (perhaps Venetian, sixteenth-century), consisting of four hinged, inlaid panels. On one side is a double board for trictrac or backgammon, running across all four panels. The two outer panels can then be folded inwards to form a board for chess or draughts, while on the other side a board for the snake game, with a fierce spiralling serpent. The board can then be folded once more, to create a compact, easily portable object. The style of the inlay decoration is broadly similar to that of the Embriachi workshop, but there are both technical and stylistic differences. There were many other workshops specializing in inlay work in Venice, where the board may have been made.**

# ARTS AND CRAFTS
# OF THE RENAISSANCE

The influence of the Renaissance, with its emphasis on the revival of ideas from the classical world, began to make itself felt in Tudor England; philosophy, literature and the arts were open to fresh interpretation as artists and scholars looked backwards to a golden age for inspiration and at the same time began to respond to new working methods that placed a premium on personal experience rather than an exclusive reliance on established texts.

**Fig. 50. STANDING MAZER,** silver-gilt and turned wood, 1529. These characteristic drinking bowls, often of bird's-eye maple, originated in the medieval period. The mounts of this sixteenth-century example are among the earliest surviving pieces of English plate with fully Renaissance ornament, while the bowl is provided with a high silver-gilt foot transforming it into a standing cup of grander proportions.

Fig. 51. LOBED BOWL of Tudor greenware. This finely potted earthenware produced on the Surrey/Hampshire border, with its bright green glaze and pleasing shape, represents a considerable refinement of the potter's craft in England

Renaissance attitudes influenced craftsmen as well as the intellectual classes. Some who had grown up in the medieval tradition of service to a master began to think of themselves as independent and original artists, more able to negotiate with a patron and to promote their own designs. Many of the painters and sculptors celebrated today as major artists had begun their working lives apprenticed to goldsmiths, where they learned how to be business-like and thrifty with materials. The medieval guild system still prevailed, but from the sixteenth century goldsmiths (among others) benefited from time-saving developments in casting series of identical components for easy assembly. At times well-known painters and sculptors would supply designs to be carried out in metalwork by the more humble craftsman, in which way everyday things such as inkwells, mustard pots, candlesticks, door-knockers and plaquettes (used to decorate furniture) might take on the status (to our eyes) of works of art. Many of these designs incorporate allusions to the iconography of classical mythology, although Christian elements also remained in demand.

The invention, in Germany, of the first domestic spring-driven clocks coincided with a remarkable growth in the quality and number of metalworkers and the developments of new skills. Both clocks and locks put a premium on accurate workman-ship: for the first time, objects that combined precision and complexity began to be relatively commonplace, and although early watches were relatively poor timekeepers the development of improved navigational instruments was a boon to sailors.

The introduction of printing increased the pace at which new styles, including ornamental motifs derived from classical prototypes, were circulated. The proliferation of new ideas available to craftsmen in the form of pattern-books may be said also to have had something of a negative influence, for widely disseminated printed pamphlets and books, led to a greater degree of standardization of ideas on a European scale. They had a tendency to limit the craftsman's full independence: his freedom to invent his own forms and to impose his own solutions on his chosen material could be compromised if his customers or patrons preferred to choose from a pattern-book.

Fig. 52. TIN-GLAZED VASE of earthenware. This ring vase, so called because of the shape of the handles has a blue glaze and is decorated with the sacred monogram *IHS*; probably it was imported from Italy. The occurrence in Oxford of such vessels, together with fine cups and mugs, suggests changing social perceptions in the city and a population with a visual awareness that may owe something to the new learning of Renaissance Europe.

Fig. 53. ALBARELLO (pharmacy jar), Hispano-Moresque. Of Islamic origin, the albarello was a common type in Spain in the fifteenth century. This type of pottery was much sought after, especially in Italy where it was greatly treasured by noble families. By the late sixteenth century this popular shape had been adopted by English delftware potters – a striking example of the way in which continental influences penetrated late Tudor England.

**Fig. 54. GLASS PLATE, Venetian, sixteenth-century.** Luxury glass such as this was imported from Venice and Antwerp. An inventory of Henry VIII's household goods drawn up in 1547 includes more than 6,000 glass vessels.

Throughout the Middle Ages the work of one ubiquitous craftsman – the potter – had enjoyed little or no artistic standing, but during the Tudor period the prestige of decorative pottery first began to be raised. An initial impulse was provided by the spread of lustre-wares made in Spain in the fourteenth and fifteenth centuries by Moorish craftsmen working for Christian masters. Particularly fine wares, made near Valencia, came to be widely exported, especially to Italy where Italian potters took up the challenge and began to produce what might be termed the first masterpieces of Renaissance ceramic art. Maiolica, as it came to be known, was the forerunner to the tin-glazed earthenware made in northern Europe but manufactured in England only from the late sixteenth century. In its early years of production this pottery known as galley-ware (later to become more familiar as the ubiquitous blue-and-white delftware) was commonly found in the form of vessels used by apothecaries to contain medicines. Other English ceramics also began to show improvements: Tudor greenwares and Cistercian-type wares for example, although

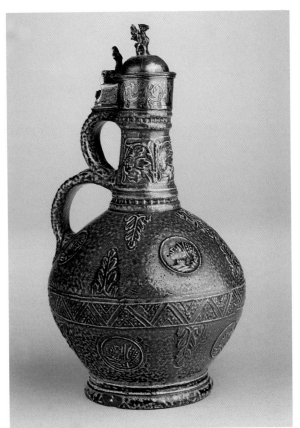

Fig. 56. SILVER-MOUNTED JUG, London 1565. Salt-glazed stoneware vessels were produced in quantities in the Rhineland and frequently were embellished with silver mounts upon importation to England.

Fig. 55. PEWTER CUP. Elaborately decorated pewter of this kind was fashionable in the late sixteenth century and early seventeenth century although very little of it now survives. This cup was made for secular use and was given to the Church at a later date.

self-coloured, displayed brighter and stronger-coloured glazes and more interesting shapes than had previously been the case.

Luxury Venetian glass was imported. The inventory compiled on the death of Henry VIII records large numbers of fine glass vessels in the royal household, some of which, at least, are believed to have been made locally in England by Venetian glass-blowers. These craftsmen are assumed to have been enticed to England, their craftsmanship being as highly prized as the imported glass which preceded them. As late as the mid-sixteenth century it remained difficult for these glass-workers to leave Venice, and indeed previously they had been under threat of death if they attempted to do so.

Decorative mounts on certain useful objects have survived recycling in the melting-pot – the fate of so much early metalwork – probably because

**Fig. 57. SILVER-GILT TANKARD, London 1574. The chased fruit and strapwork and the engraved and stamped decoration of this tankard is typical of the repetitive nature of most late Elizabethan plate. The tapering, cylindrical form of the body probably derives from early drinking vessels made of horn.**

of the small amounts of precious metal retrievable. Mazers and stoneware jugs are a case in point. The former, a type of bowl of turned wood, was made deeper and more elaborate by the addition of a deep, silver-gilt lip, which might be chased or engraved; by the Renaissance period vessels of medieval origin had been transformed into standing cups. Stoneware ceramics were to become more prevalent in England in the Stuart period, but imported examples from Germany in the second quarter of the sixteenth century eloquently illustrate the high value

placed upon them (compared to indigenous earthenwares) by the decorative silver-gilt mounts with which they are commonly embellished.

Craftsmen were inevitably influenced by imports from abroad and by immigrants working in England. By the end of the Tudor period, many of the more tangible manifestations of continental Renaissance taste had been thoroughly absorbed into the fabric of English craftsmanship, while centuries of independent tradition ensured that it retained its independent stamp.

# BIBILOGRAPHY

G. R. Elton, 1955. *England under the Tudors* (London).

E. Hawkins, 1885. *Medallic Illustrations of the History of Great Britain and Ireland* (London).

D. D. Boyden, 1969. *The Hill Collection of Musical Instruments in the Ashmolean Museum, Oxford* (Oxford).

W. G. Hoskins, 1955. *The Making of the English Landscape* (London).

J. Laver, 1969. *A Concise History of Costume* (Norwich).

D. Scarisbrick, 1995. *Tudor and Jacobean Jewellery* (Tate Gallery, London).

T. Schroder, 1988. *English Domestic Silver 1500-1900* (London).

P. J. Seaby, 1985. *The Story of British Coinage* (London).

D. Starkey, (ed.), 1991. *Henry VIII; A European Court In England* (London).

——, 1998. *The Inventory of King Henry VIII* (London).

J. Thirsk (ed.), 1967. *The Agrarian History of England and Wales 1500-1640* (Cambridge).

R. Walker, 1997. *Miniatures (A selection of miniatures in the Ashmolean Museum)* (Oxford).

# ILLUSTRATIONS